BETWE S

BY JOE HORTUA

★

★

DRAMATISTS
PLAY SERVICE
INC.

BETWEEN US
Copyright © 2008, Joe Hortua

All Rights Reserved

SPECIAL NOTE

For Beth

BETWEEN US was originally commissioned by South Coast Repertory Theatre in 2002.

BETWEEN US received its world premiere at Manhattan Theatre Club (Lynne Meadow, Artistic Director; Barry Grove, Executive Producer) in New York City on April 20, 2004. It was directed by Christopher Ashley; the set design was by Neil Patel; the costume design was by Jess Goldstein; the lighting design was by Christopher Akerlind; and the sound design was by Darron L. West. The cast was as follows:

JOEL .... David Harbour
SHARYL .... Kate Jennings Grant
CARLO .... Bradley White
GRACE. .... Daphne Rubin-Vega

BETWEEN US received its West Coast premiere at the Met Theatre in Los Angeles, California, in May 2005. It was directed by Alejandro Furth. The cast was as follows:

JOEL .... Andrew Hamrick
SHARYL .... Lisa Welti
CARLO .... Ruben Gonzalez
GRACE .... Onahoua Rodriguez

CHARACTERS

GRACE — 30s
CARLO — 30s
JOEL — 30s
SHARYL — 30s

SETTING

Act One — A suburb in the Midwest.
Act Two — New York City, years later.

NOTES

A forward slash (/) indicates the point at which the following character's dialogue begins to overlap. Two or more forward slashes (//) at a point indicate that two or more of the *following* characters' dialogue begin simultaneously at this point.

BETWEEN US

ACT ONE

1999. After dinner. A living room in a luxurious home. Neatly in one corner, some industrial buckets, two-by-fours and contracting equipment. Joel and Sharyl are hosting. Joel is slightly slumped in chair. Sharyl stands, pouring wine. Carlo and Grace sit on a couch. All the characters are in their thirties.

GRACE. Then he says ...
CARLO. Are you telling them the part?
GRACE. As if he's reliving some memory.
CARLO. The lust part.
GRACE. As if he's recalling — what part?
CARLO. The part about lust ...
GRACE. Yeah, yeah.
JOEL. Lust?
CARLO. We froze ...
GRACE. Looking at our priest. And he's looking out the window. As if / he's remembering / something long ago.
CARLO. Yeah. Lost.
GRACE. Says of course one can *lust* at first / sight.
CARLO. "Lust at first sight."
GRACE. Of course of course one can *lust* at first / sight.
JOEL. A priest says / this?
CARLO. Our / priest. Father ... what was it?
SHARYL. What a priest.
GRACE. Father Whatever. Says ... Everyone has physical reactions, / says. Everyone will gape at a white neck.
SHARYL. Noooo, he / doesn't.
GRACE. Oh yes.

7

CARLO. He said *milky*.

GRACE. What? Fine. A milky white neck.

CARLO. Just milky. Not white.

GRACE. A milky neck.

CARLO. A milky neck.

JOEL. The Father says this?

CARLO. *(Shrugs.)* What can I say? Poetic priest.

GRACE. The gape of a milky neck. A beautiful lock of hair. Or the pink of warm flesh. Warm flesh, his words.

SHARYL. Pink!

JOEL. No!

CARLO. It's true!

JOEL. The poor guy hasn't gotten any in years!

CARLO. I guess not.

JOEL. Well I know what *that's* like! *(Grace, Carlo and Joel laugh. Sharyl smiles.)*

GRACE. And we're stunned. Stu/nned. I / mean, what? What is this Catholic / priest saying? Then he starts in on. What was it?

CARLO. Stunned.

JOEL. Of course.

CARLO. Stunned. The Great Com/panion.

GRACE. THE GREAT COMPANION OF YOUR LIFE!

CARLO. And / something about Tolstoy. And / being on your deathbed. And a unit ...

SHARYL. The *what?*

GRACE. From a Tolstoy book. Morphed into / one.

CARLO. Morphed.

GRACE. Morphed into one.

CARLO. A unit morphed into one.

GRACE. Then Carlo offered him our first born. *(Pause.)* Well did you or didn't you?

CARLO. I had to sign a paper saying / I would.

GRACE. It was *all* fun / until then.

CARLO. Yeah yeah, the recovering Catholic had to make things difficult.

GRACE. Ex-Catholic not recovering.

CARLO. Religion, the one thing that makes this one nervy and difficult.

GRACE. Asks us. You two were raised Catholic. Why won't you

marry in / a church? Suddenly he gets very paternal with me. Don't you believe / in …

CARLO. Does not.

GRACE. Does. Don't you believe in God? Says / to me. Don't you believe in God, *young lady?* So / I say. Of course I believe in God, Father … Whatever. It's not that I don't / believe in God. I do. I do believe in Him. It's just that He's become impossible. So I'm turning my back on Him. And walking away.

CARLO. He didn't say it like that.

JOEL. Oh boy.

CARLO. She exaggerates. He thought you were sooo funny.

JOEL. Heathen!

SHARYL. You didn't?

CARLO. Nice, huh? Funny joke, huh?

GRACE. Who said it was a joke?

CARLO. We were there to get the priest. For my parents.

GRACE. I should've whipped out my birth control on his desk.

CARLO. You're so funny.

GRACE. So Carlo had to / vow. That he must do … "EVERY-THING IN HIS POWER" To raise HIS children / Catholic.

CARLO. The paper said "our" children.

GRACE. Did it?

CARLO. It was just a paper.

GRACE. It was our spine. *(Carlo shoots her a look. Pause. She decides to be nice and kiss him on the head.)*

CARLO. What are *you two* smirking about? You're both Catholic.

JOEL. The only thing Catholic left in me is my love of the Sistine Chapel.

GRACE. Well, the priest was sweet.

CARLO. He got loaded.

GRACE. Priests aren't forbidden from getting loaded. I'm sure he has stress like the rest of us. He *was* a very sweet drunk. I actually danced with him.

JOEL. He danced?

CARLO. Disgusting.

GRACE. He put his hands on my *hips! (Joel and Sharyl burst out laughing. Then Grace. Then finally Carlo smiles and shakes his head.)* He wasn't a *bad* dancer. Seriously. It was fun.

CARLO. The whole thing was *horrendous.* Everyone was laughing at him and he had no idea. It was so embarrassing, it was beyond irony. The whole reception made a circle around them. Her in white. Him in black. The DJ playing into it. My poor mother couldn't believe / her eyes.

GRACE. Oh she laughed. Your mother / laughed.

CARLO. She did not!

GRACE. She did.

CARLO. My mother was / appalled.

GRACE. *She* even danced / with him.

CARLO. Are you // crazy?

JOEL. Liddy!

GRACE. *Everyone* danced / with the priest.

CARLO. It was *your* mother who / danced with him!

GRACE. Well, my mother *would*, wouldn't /she?

JOEL. Liddy did not dance with the priest, did she?

CARLO. My mother *did not* dance / with the priest.

GRACE. Boohoo. She did too. I saw her.

SHARYL. Speaking of mothers. My mother-in-law will be calling sometime tonight. We can all look forward to it. I apologize in advance. *(Grace smiles and waves it off.)*

CARLO. *(Puzzled.)* Did my mother really … *(Slight pause.)* Did she dance with the priest? *(Pause. Grace smiles and nods yes.)* It was revolting. This sweaty balding priest. Laughing and dancing with twenty-something bridesmaids.

JOEL. Well, I'm sweaty and balding. And *I* would love to dance with twenty-something bridesmaids.

SHARYL. Well that's nothing new, Joel.

CARLO. You're balding?

JOEL. I am.

CARLO. Where?

JOEL. Where? What do you mean where? Where does anyone bald?

CARLO. Let me see. *(Carlo looks.)* It's all over for you.

JOEL. Thanks. It's been over for me for years. Ask her.

SHARYL. Very funny, Joel.

JOEL. She reminds me of it. Every night before we go to bed. *(They all laugh. Sharyl doesn't.)* Oh Sharyl. Please. *Relax. (Pause.)* Speaking of drunk balding men. Let's let this one make a toast. *(They raise their glasses.)* To the / two of you and your wedding. Sorry to have missed it. Seems like yesterday, Carlo. Both in New York. Photographers in grad school. Such dreams. And look at us now.

Settled. Starting families. It's like we're different people. I'm sorry we missed your / wedding. Events like weddings shouldn't be missed. They are what give life meaning, belonging, joy, / community.

SHARYL. Here we go. Yes, sorry. Oh Joel don't be such a drunk ham.

JOEL. She often calls me / that, a drunk ham.

SHARYL. Well, often, you *are* a drunk ham.

JOEL. I still don't know exactly what she *means* / by it.

SHARYL. I *mean* you're *sentimental* when / you're drunk.

JOEL. *Anyway. (Turns to Carlo and Grace.)* To the two of you, Carlo and Grace. To your future. Love. Success. Fortune. We love you. We think you're the best. We really do.

CARLO. Thank you.

GRACE. Thank you guys. *(They all clink glasses. Sharyl discreetly avoids Joel's glass. They drink.)*

JOEL. How are your photos coming?

CARLO. Great, actually.

JOEL. Good.

CARLO. I have two exhibits this year.

JOEL. Where?

CARLO. Blott Gallery. And at Hasselbanks.

JOEL. Really? Hasselbanks?

CARLO. You should see what else they have lined up at Hasselbanks / for the Spring.

JOEL. I've read about the Romario ...

CARLO. The Romario / Restrospective.

JOEL. Right.

CARLO. You know his / work?

JOEL. Italian. Large metallic prints.

CARLO. You have to come and see it with me. You would love his / work.

JOEL. I *do* love it. I ...

CARLO. I can't believe my name is on a brochure with Romario. I'll be hanging out with him, / you know. It's been quite a whirl-wind / these past few months.

JOEL. Really? Sure. Well, you deserve it.

GRACE. *(Reaching in her bag.)* You want a copy of the brochure?

JOEL. Of course.

CARLO. Grace.

GRACE. What? I brought them one.

CARLO. She carries these brochures around with her. *(Grace hands over the big glossy brochure to Joel. Joel opens it. They all stand over Joel as he flips slowly, page to page.)*

GRACE. The magazine *Blind Spot.* Is doing an article on him this coming Spring. We'll send you a copy.

JOEL. I still have a subscription.

SHARYL. Look at that. I like that one. *(He continues to flip through the pages, slowly.)* And that one too.

JOEL. How did you do that?

CARLO. Basically gum printing. Just a diluted, strange solution mix. *(Finishes the last print. Closes the brochure.)*

JOEL. *(Undoubtedly impressed and earnest.)* These … are pretty amazing Carlo. This is gonna be a breakthrough for you.

CARLO. We'll see.

GRACE. He sold three last week. And / he has a commission.

JOEL. Great.

CARLO. I'm also doing some / new things with lith printing.

GRACE. For the lobby of the Giggs Hotel.

JOEL. The Giggs.

SHARYL. Now, *that's* a nice hotel.

JOEL. *Wow,* Carlo

CARLO. Yeah.

JOEL. Wonderful.

CARLO. It's about time. The waiting and waiting. It was terrifying. You know, Del Piero has really helped out.

JOEL. *Professor Max Del Piero.* I haven't thought of him in ages. God, I hated that pretentious prick.

CARLO. You hated him. Because he didn't like *your* work.

JOEL. Well, he loved *your* work.

CARLO. His agent picked me up.

JOEL. Cynthia Ballak?

CARLO. Yep.

JOEL. Good God. You're in the big time now.

CARLO. I did a series on children. Playing house. Making dinner. Going to bed. Arguing in living rooms. Smoking. Posed just like adults.

JOEL. I could see why Del Piero would love that. *(Pause.)*

GRACE. It was beautiful.

CARLO. I'm very proud of it. *(Pause.)*

SHARYL. And you Grace. Are you still managing the restaurant?

GRACE. Mm. Hopefully not much longer. I think I want to go to graduate school.

SHARYL. Really? In what?

GRACE. Probably social work.

SHARYL. Wow.

GRACE. We'll see.

JOEL. Honorable.

CARLO. A social worker with an art photographer. Debtor's prison awaits.

JOEL. Well, there are worse places to end up.

SHARYL. I didn't know you were interested in social work.

GRACE. I am.

SHARYL. Didn't you do communications in undergrad?

GRACE. It was a joke degree.

SHARYL. Oh come on now.

GRACE. What? You guys got real degrees. At real schools.

JOEL. Oh did we?

CARLO. Grace always talks down her undergrad degree.

GRACE. Oh right. *(Points to Joel.)* Dartmouth. *(Points to Carlo.)* Wesleyan. *(Points to Sharyl.)* Cornell. *(Points to herself.)* Hofstra!

JOEL. Grace. If it's any consolation. I learned my worst habits. *(Toasts.)* At Darmouth.

SHARYL. *(Seemingly genuine, but not completely.)* Well Grace. I think it's all great.

GRACE. Thanks. It's a good time for us, I think.

JOEL. Just beware of giving social services. With those legs.

CARLO. *(Kisses her cheek.)* Don't worry. I'll make her wear slacks. Baggy and woolen.

GRACE. Whatever I wear. I probably won't look attractive.

JOEL. Oh? Why's that? *(Grace looks at Carlo. They smile awkwardly.)*

SHARYL. What? Are you —

GRACE. No. Not yet. But ... maybe / while I go back to school.

JOEL. *(Eyes widen.)* Oooo *babies.*

CARLO. Just speculation right now.

JOEL. *(To Sharyl.)* Do you remember when we used to do that, Sharyl?

SHARYL. Are you trying?

CARLO. We're not, not trying.

JOEL. *(To Sharyl.)* Do you remember when we used to do that, Sharyl?

SHARYL. Excuse me?

JOEL. Do you remember when we …

SHARYL. *(Quickly, stony.)* When we *what*? *(Slight pause.)*

JOEL. *(Innocently.)* Speculated? *(Joel toasts her with a gentle smile.)*

GRACE. And you, Sharyl?

SHARYL. *(Swallows wine. Caught off guard. Turns to Grace.)* Me?

GRACE. Are you working?

SHARYL. No. *(Slight pause. Smiles.)* I'm with the baby for now.

GRACE. Enjoying it?

SHARYL. *(Puzzled by the question. Smiles.)* I think so.

CARLO. Good. *(Silence.)*

JOEL. Well, you're both doing it. You're / really doing it. It's inspiring. And what's better. You're doing it/ your own way.

CARLO. I don't know about *that*. Please.

JOEL. No no. It's true. You are. And when biographies are written of Carlo. I will be part of the drunken early years.

CARLO. The biographies will be written about *you*.

JOEL. Yes, my work in advertising.

GRACE. The early years. Good God, you two / were crazy then.

CARLO. Those were drunken years, weren't they?

JOEL. They still are. For some. *(Joel grins and toasts. They all drink.)*

SHARYL. Well, it's good to see both of you.

CARLO. Thanks.

GRACE. Yes, thank you. *(Offstage, the baby cries.)*

SHARYL. I'll be right back. *(Sharyl leaves.)*

JOEL. Give him the Chubby Snubby. A brown bear. He loves / it.

SHARYL. *(Offstage.)* I know he loves / it.

JOEL. I was talking to *them*.

SHARYL. *(Offstage.)* What?

JOEL. I was / talking to *them*.

SHARYL. *(Offstage.)* What?

JOEL. I WAS TALKING …

SHARYL. *(Offstage.)* *I* introduced the Chubby Snubby to him.

JOEL. *(To Grace and Carlo.)* I bought it actually.

SHARYL. *(Offstage.)* You bought it. And threw it at him. I've actually played with him with the bear. Besides. The Chubby Snubby is dead. *(Sharyl comes down the stairs.)* I closed the door. He'll cry himself to sleep. *(Sharyl opens her mouth about to speak and the phone rings.)* Ah. Mom-in-law. *(Sharyl smiles sarcastically and*

14

answers. To phone.) Hellooooo?

JOEL. What do you mean the Chubby Snubby is dead?

SHARYL. *(To phone.)* We're having people / over for dinner.

JOEL. Since …

SHARYL. No, of course, we're not bothered / but we just …

JOEL. When did this … *(Sharyl stops him. Listens.)*

SHARYL. *(Bluntly.)* I do have to go though, Mom. *(Sharyl listens.)*

JOEL. Since when is he dead?

CARLO. *(Chuckling.)* Jesus, this dead teddy bear is really upsetting you, Joel. *(Grace and Carlo laugh. Joel stares at them, doesn't laugh. Looks back to Sharyl. Sharyl listens more. And more. And more.)*

SHARYL. *(To Joel.)* Take the phone.

JOEL. You killed his Chubby Snubby?

SHARYL. Yes, I ate the Chubby Snubby. Now please take the phone. *(To phone.)* What? Yes. The Chubby Snubby. Right. The one with the bow. *(Rolls her eyes.)* We took the Chubby Snubby to the Salvation Army. We said bye bye to it.

GRACE. *(Joking like a little girl.)* Bye bye. *(Carlo turns to Grace. Grace giggles.)*

JOEL. The Chubby Snubby was fine.

SHARYL. *(To phone.)* Joel had a…? *(To Joel.)* You had a Chubby Snubby.

JOEL. What was that thing called?

SHARYL. Bing Bing.

GRACE. Bing Bing.

JOEL. Right. Had this little bell. Ask her if she still has Bing Bing somewhere? *(Carlo looks at Grace. Grace giggles.)*

CARLO. How much wine have you had?

GRACE. *(Shrugs.)* Just enough. *(Carlo and Grace laugh sweetly. Grace lays her head on Carlo's shoulder.)*

SHARYL. *(To phone.)* It was *our* name. We — We made it — Can I talk, Mom? *(Pause.)* We made the name up.

JOEL. Does she still have / that Bing Bing?

SHARYL. Shush.

JOEL. Ask her if she still / has it.

SHARYL. *(Exasperated.)* Do you still have his Bing Bing? *(Rolls eyes. To Joel.)* Of course she … *(To phone.)* Oh. I shouldn't have thrown the Chubby out? Well thank you, MOM. *(To Joel. Hands phone out.)* Deal with her.

JOEL. I don't feel like talking. *(Sharyl drops the phone on the couch.*

All four of them stare at it. Silence. Joel slowly picks it up. Curtly, swiftly, quietly.) Hi Mom. Can I call you back tomorrow? Bye. *(Joel hangs up the phone quietly. Joel stares at Sharyl.)* So you threw out his …

SHARYL. SHUT UP WITH GODDAM CHUBBY SNUBBY! *(Silence. They all stare at Sharyl. Joel opens the window.)* It's freezing cold out, Joel.

JOEL. Are you two warm?

GRACE. I'm fine.

SHARYL. I'm cold. *(Sharyl shuts the window. Long awkward silence.)*

CARLO. So … how are things at work?

JOEL. Abysmal.

CARLO. What are you working on?

JOEL. You don't want to know.

CARLO. No, tell me.

JOEL. Last month. For some photos. I spent four hundred billable hours. Worrying about. Getting honey. To drip just right. Off of a granola bar.

CARLO. Well, you're obviously very successful at it. *(Awkward silence. Grace looks at Joel, then Sharyl, grins sweetly.)*

GRACE. I like this wine. *(Pause.)*

JOEL. *(Chuckles.)* Sharyl, she / likes it.

SHARYL. Is that funny to you?

JOEL. We had a little discussion earlier / today about it.

SHARYL. All right, Joel, / stop.

JOEL. Sharyl in her good mood. Blindly picked / it out of the cellar this morning.

SHARYL. *(Sighs.)* Joel?

GRACE. You have a cellar?

JOEL. Oh yeah. Sharyl loves it. It's her favorite room / of the house.

SHARYL. You really are going to spoil the night / aren't you?

JOEL. *(Eyes light up.)* Dark. Damp. Dirty. She poured our wine into her Waterford decanter today. Which I find ridiculous / and pretentious, by the way. Because if you know anything / about wines. You only decant something that needs air. But not Sharyl. She / decants ALL OF THEM.

SHARYL. He's drunk.

CARLO. Joel. Joel?

JOEL. It's true. That decanter stands for *everything*. And so I was curious what we were going to drink this evening. And I asked her

16

where she grabbed it from. Because I actually know a thing about wines. I have them organized in the cellar. Spanish to the left. Napa's around the bend. Bordeaux's front and center. And Sharyl's white Zins in a shitty corner beneath everything. So I asked her. Where did you get it. And she said. In the lovely way she's known for. *(Witchy voice.)* HOW THE HELL DO I KNOW, *JOEL*, I JUST GRABBED ONE! *(Pause.)* And I pressed further. Well, darling. Please. Think. Visualize the corner you plucked it from. And do you know what she said? She said. Just like this. *(Leans forward. Witchy voice.)* HELL'S CORNER! *(Everyone looks perplexed.)* Exactly. *(Joel laughs.)* We could either be drinking. A hundred-dollar bottle of Ruffino. Or cooking wine. *(Pause.)*

GRACE. You really have a wine cellar?

JOEL. Copper pots in the kitchen. Persian rugs in each room. Marble bathtubs.

GRACE. The house is beautiful.

JOEL. You think?

SHARYL. Thank you.

GRACE. So much space.

SHARYL. I'm happy / with how it turned out.

JOEL. Lots of space.

SHARYL. Can we talk?

JOEL. If you're not used to so much space. It can make you anxious.

CARLO. Anxious?

JOEL. You see that large plant? There's all this *free space* around it. I want to fill it. The sight of it nags me. Sometimes I even take something. And move / it. *(Joel drags fern along the wooden floor.)*

CARLO. Easy there, big guy.

JOEL. Just to fill that space. But then of course. The space I moved it from is now empty. So I put it back. *(Kicks the fern back. Long silence. Sharyl quietly returns the fern. Stares into Joel's eyes. No one knows what to say.)*

GRACE. Well you'll just have to buy more things! *(Sharyl and Joel do not laugh.)*

CARLO. New job. Good money. That's what you moved here for, right? For a better environment. More space. Children. Grass. A driveway. *(Joel huffs sarcastically.)*

GRACE. Don't you like it out here?

SHARYL. I like it.

JOEL. You're originally from the Midwest, right Carlo?

CARLO. Hey. I warned you. No paradise. But —

JOEL. The cold. Good God!

CARLO. The cold is uninhabitable.

JOEL. And the people!

CARLO. Nice, no? *(Slight pause.)*

JOEL. HORRIBLE! Have you ever noticed. When you ask people from these uninhabitable places. What makes this part of the country so special. They say it's *the people.* The people. The people are friendly. The people are good. The people are nice. Do you know *why* they say that? BECAUSE THERE'S NOTHING ELSE HERE! *(Raises the blinds. Flat dreary landscape.)* Whenever there's a lack of anything decent. You can always rely on "the good people." Ice-cold winters, gray skies, mosquito summers. But the people are good. The sport teams are good. That touchdown last week was good. *DRESDEN* AFTER *WORLD WAR TWO* HAD MORE TO DO THAN THIS WASTELAND! There's nothing, I mean, *NOTHING* to do! But we have our painted faces. And our football. And our sausages. And our *people. (Awkward silence.)*

GRACE. Well you have a *beautiful* house now.

SHARYL. Thank you.

GRACE. It feels so new.

SHARYL. Sorry to have you sleep / in the living room.

GRACE. Oh please it's / fine!

SHARYL. The whole second floor is being / remodeled.

GRACE. We're just happy to see you. *(Pause.)*

SHARYL. Well, it's nice to have you. *(Offstage, we hear a child crying.)* Excuse me again. *(Sharyl goes up the stairs. Silence.)*

CARLO. So tell me more about your job.

JOEL. No. *(Silence.)*

GRACE. I'll go and see the baby.

JOEL. You don't have to le ... okay. *(Grace goes up the stairs. Silence. Carlo doesn't know what to do as Joel broods. Carlo looks at baby photo on a table. Points at it to Joel. Smiles. Joel tightly grins. Looks down at his stomach.)*

CARLO. Twenty pounds.

JOEL. Um?

CARLO. *(Turns, holding his paunch.)* Look at this. *(Pause.)* Does it get worse when you have a kid? *(Joel looks at him. Silence. Then Joel chuckles. Ruffles his own hair. Smears his palms along his eyes.)* So tell me, man. *(Pause. Joel raises his eyebrows, waiting.)* What's it like having a child? *(Joel looks at Carlo, then sadly and quietly looks into his drink.)*

JOEL. Yesterday. I rolled around with Lucien for an hour. Kissed his neck. His nose. His ears. *(Looks up at Carlo. Smiles.)* He laughed. And he squirmed. And I laughed. And I squirmed. Then in one sudden moment, as I tickled him, he squealed … and sunk his teeth into my shoulder. *(Pulls his collar, showing Carlo a bite mark.)* That's what it's like having a kid. *(Pause. Joel shrugs. Carlo looks out the window.)*

CARLO. Remember that argument we had?

JOEL. Argument?

CARLO. *(Shakes his head.)* God, the things we argued about in grad school. Embarrassing.

JOEL. Which? We had many.

CARLO. Kids. Whether or not / to have them.

JOEL. Ah.

CARLO. I said I was ambivalent. I wouldn't jeopardize a career. By thoughtlessly having a child. Because I was supposed to. Because it was expected of me. Because it's just what you do. And you said I was just being difficult. That I was arguing for the sake of arguing. That one day I would change my mind. And I called you simple and naïve and sentimental. We were drunk on pitchers of cheap beer.

JOEL. I called you a fake.

CARLO. Actually, you called me a phony.

JOEL. *(Smiles.)* It really pissed you off.

CARLO. I said if you ever called me that again. I would take a swing at you.

JOEL. Authenticity meant everything then.

CARLO. It got nasty. I took a step forward to you. *(Steps closer.)*

JOEL. And then I called you a phony again.

CARLO. And I put my fist out. *(Pause.)* Like I was going to hit you … *(Carlo smiles. Joel then smiles.)*

JOEL. And then we both burst out laughing. *(They smile at each other. Then stare at the ground. Joel stares into his drink, in stony pain.)*

CARLO. You were right?

JOEL. *(Not looking up.)* Was I?

CARLO. I've changed my mind. I want a big family. Like the one I grew up in. Things seems meaningless without children.

JOEL. Things don't necessarily become meaningful. Because you have children.

CARLO. If not meaningful. What?

JOEL. Oh, I don't want to have this conversation, Carlo. *(Pause. Carlo is taken back.)* Don't try to cheer me up.

CARLO. Fine.

JOEL. Or ask me to repeat clichés that parents pass around like cocktail napkins.

CARLO. Okay, Joel.

JOEL. "Kids are a lot of work but they're worth it." "Your life changes so much." "You learn so much about yourself." "I can't imagine my life without them." "My son teaches me more than I teach him." "They grow up *so* fast." To be honest. It's more exhausting to prop up these conversations. Than it is to *actually* have kids.

CARLO. I was just talking.

JOEL. I'm just fumbling through it like the next guy. Just like you will. Just like our fathers and mothers. Like everyone. We should all stop self-consciously chatting about parenthood. It doesn't do any good really. I mean, do you hear apes at the zoo rambling on about their offspring? And what they *mean* to them? And what they've learned? And how their lives have changed?

CARLO. Am I an ape now?

JOEL. You tell me?

CARLO. Are you an ape? *(Joel beats his chest and screams like an ape. The two women enter and stare at the men.)*

SHARYL. More wine anyone?

JOEL. Yes, thanks.

SHARYL. I don't think you want / any more, Joel.

JOEL. I don't?

SHARYL. No.

JOEL. I thought I just asked you / for more.

SHARYL. But I don't think you *really* want / any more.

JOEL. Oh is that / right?

SHARYL. Do you really want / more?

JOEL. What do you think, / Sharyl?

SHARYL. I just told you / what I thought.

JOEL. I'd like some more wine / for God's sake.

SHARYL. Why didn't you get yourself some while I was gone, if you wanted / more wine?

CARLO. Guys, guys *stop* it will you? *(Pause. They consider stopping.)*

JOEL. It didn't strike me, Sharyl.

SHARYL. What didn't / strike you?

JOEL. The thought.

SHARYL. Do you want more?

JOEL. Fill me, darling. *(Sharyl doesn't and puts down the bottle. Joel gets up and exits. Sharyl picks up the bottle.)*

SHARYL. More? *(Carlo nods no. Grace accepts. Grace touches Sharyl's arm. Sharyl gently recoils.)*

GRACE. Should we…?

SHARYL. Of course you shouldn't. *(Joel enters with a bottle of scotch and a rocks glass. Joel sits and pours himself a neat scotch.)*

JOEL. Scotch anyone? *(Silence. No response.)*

CARLO. I was just telling Joel I've gained twenty pounds.

SHARYL. Really? Where? *(Carlo bowls out his abdomen.)* That's disgusting. *(Sharyl playfully touches it.)*

CARLO. *(Patting his stomach.)* She's right. It is disgusting.

JOEL. Now now.

SHARYL. And we're just about to have dessert.

CARLO. Dessert?

SHARYL. Crème brûlées.

GRACE. Carlo's favorite.

SHARYL. Remember when you took us to Le Fou?

GRACE. Right, for your / anniversary, Le Fou.

CARLO. Fantastic brûlées at Le Fou.

SHARYL. And the waiter spilled coffee on Joel. *(They all laugh. Joel wryly toasts.)*

GRACE. My God. Le Fou. It's been a while. And we live two blocks away!

SHARYL. You don't go?

GRACE. We try not to eat out as much.

CARLO. Yeah, right. Instead of five nights a week. Three or four. The credit card companies love us.

JOEL. Nothing like Le Fou out here. Just steak houses. Sausage factories. And slaughter houses. *(Pause.)*

CARLO. Well, thank you, Sharyl, for / the crème brûlée.

GRACE. Yes, thank you, it's / very thoughtful.

SHARYL. Well, don't thank me *yet*.

CARLO. I'm sure it's even better than Le Fou's.

SHARYL. Were you always so ingratiating?

JOEL. Another toast. *(Toasts.)* Age earns us our imperfections. *(They clink glasses and drink.)*

SHARYL. What the hell sort of toast was *that?*

JOEL. So don't worry about it, Carlo.

CARLO. Worry about?

JOEL. Age. Bellies, / baldness. Kids.

CARLO. *(Chuckles.)* Oh, right.

JOEL. You never want to get too perfect.

CARLO. Me. *(Smiles and toasts. Keeping it light.)* Sure I do.

SHARYL. Joel means. Don't try to be too happy. It would upset him.

JOEL. Sharyl / Sharyl Sharyl.

SHARYL. It would actually make him reconsider. How miserable he is. Really, it would.

JOEL. *(Sarcastic.)* It would.

SHARYL. It's better for him to sulk and act out like a toddler.

JOEL. *(Sarcastic.)* It is. You've caught us at a bad time. Sharyl and I have been, well, how would you describe it, Sharyl?

SHARYL. We're getting a divorce. Let's have dessert. *(Sharyl exits. Then reenters with a tray of crème brûlées and a butane burner. She lights the butane burner for the crème brûlées.)*

CARLO. What? You're kidding right?

JOEL. Are we kidding Sharyl?

SHARYL. No. *(Sharyl starts torching the tops of the crème brûlées. Looks up. Continues torching.)*

CARLO. But. You. You were.

JOEL. What?

CARLO. So happy.

JOEL. Were we?

CARLO. We stood at your wedding.

GRACE. We had plans. Next summer. Our vacation in Costa Rica.

SHARYL. Well, we're not divorcing to inconvenience you. *(Pause.)*

GRACE. You could see a counselor.

JOEL. A counselor? Please. A referee.

GRACE. But that beautiful boy. Sleeping in there. What's going to happen ... *(Pause.)*

CARLO. Are you serious? *(Pause.)*

JOEL. That couch you're / sitting on.

SHARYL. Okay, Joel.

JOEL. It's a pull-out bed.

SHARYL. Enough.

JOEL. I have a feeling my name is embroidered / on it somewhere.

SHARYL. It's getting old, Joel. The joke is / getting old.

JOEL. *(Looking under a seat cushion.)* Who said it was / a joke?

SHARYL. Your sarcasm is getting very / old.

JOEL. She ordered it last year / *as a pull-out couch.*

SHARYL. Joel thinks I ordered it / just for him.

JOEL. We've never had a pull-out couch in our lives! Not even in our little apartment in New York! And she / orders a pull-out couch. *HERE?* You see. Sharyl claims to be *above* my nasty / words. But Sharyl fights in very subtle ways. I refuse to sleep on it. I have a little / mattress in / one of the guest rooms. I sleep amongst the timber and / drywall. I think I'm becoming asthmatic because of it. But I refuse to even *sit* on that / couch. Because if I do. She wins.

SHARYL. You're ridiculous. Look at the way you're behaving.

CARLO. Guys. Okay, Joel. This. This is too much.

JOEL. Too much? This? This is *nothing. (Pause.)*

GRACE. We don't mind the couch.

JOEL. *Good,* it's all yours.

SHARYL. *(Gets close to Joel.)* I'm asking you to stop now. *(Silence.)*

JOEL. My wife has a Brazilian lover half her age. *(Sharyl slowly closes her eyes, then turns to Joel.)*

SHARYL. Are you going to ruin the whole evening?

JOEL. Just broken up with her.

SHARYL. *(Steely eyed.)* Goddam you.

JOEL. She doesn't leave the house anymore at four in the afternoon! She used to leave / the house at four! Right on the nose! Four o'clock!

GRACE. Carlo.

JOEL. Basso Nova Brasilero! That's what I call him! I used to play our Basso Nova CDs! To get a rise / out of Sharyl! Then she threw them out! So / I bought some more! Then she found those! And threw those / out! So I bought more! Back and forth! Like this for months!

CARLO. Joel.

SHARYL. You *asshole.*

CARLO. Stop. *(Getting up.)* Okay let's go, Grace.

JOEL. Go? GO WHERE? Look! You're in the *fucking* Tundra! *(Pause.)*

SHARYL. *(Getting close to him.)* I'm asking you nicely please *sto —*

JOEL. Basso Nova dumped my wife. And because of that. I have to watch her mope around in her robe in this vacuous palace of shit.

SHARYL. Maybe when I'm around you I *intuitively* mope.

JOEL. Oh, your Brazilian depression is *my* / fault then?

SHARYL. *(Her voice steadily rising.) Depression?* Who said / anything about depression? I'm talking about moping. I guess what I'm saying, *Joel.* Is that I am not *really* moping. Because / I don't have anything to really mope about. I'm / quite *satisfied*, is what I mean. *(Pause. Sharyl stares deeply into Joel's eyes. A cold, steeling stare.)* How do you know he was my only? *(It slowly sinks into Joel.)*

JOEL. "Only"?

SHARYL. Basso. Nova. *(Pause. Joel awkwardly laughs.)*

JOEL. *(Saving face.)* That's clever, Sharyl.

SHARYL. What is?

JOEL. That's really cl —

SHARYL. Really w*hat?* Tell me? What? What's clever? *(Silence.)* You're smug. But the truth is you know nothing. And I will never tell you what you want to know. *(Silence.)*

JOEL. One day I'm going to murder you. *(Sharyl gets close to him and stares him directly in the eyes.)*

SHARYL. I look forward to it. *(Turns to Carlo and Grace.)* Crème brûlées anyone? *(No response. Carlo and Grace sit shell-shocked.)*

GRACE. I feel sick. *(Sharyl starts to clean up. Joel's eyes water in anger and pain.)*

SHARYL. Joel was tanked before you even / got here.

JOEL. What do you mean / by "only"?

SHARYL. *(Speaking over him.)* We really don't socialize much anymore. Joel / has the habit of embarrassing us.

JOEL. Sharyl? What do you *mean* by —

SHARYL. It's one of the reasons we didn't come to your wedding. I'm sorry you had to see this.

JOEL. It'll do them good to see what a marriage can become!

SHARYL. *(Grabs Joel's wrist from Carlo. Steely eyed.)* IT WILL DO THEM GOOD TO KNOW THAT *I FIND YOU ABOMINABLE!* THAT THE *THOUGHT* OF HAVING *SEX* WITH YOU *REVOLTS* ME! *(Stares closely into his eyes, with a quiet seriousness.)* I would rather you see a *whore*, than have you even put your hands on my shoulders. *(Sharyl goes to the window. Looks out. Then turns to Joel. Even quieter, but with pure hatred.)* My stomach churns at the thought of our wedding day. *(Joel throws the bottle at her. Sharyl flinches to her right. The bottle sails past her and goes through a window. Silence. Joel exits. Sharyl starts to cry quietly. Grace goes to her. Sharyl stops her with her hand. Grace looks at Carlo, who inspects the window. Then back at Sharyl. Then at Carlo again. Grace sits. Graces stands.*

Graces sits again. This time longer. Grace stands. Sits again. Puts her face in her palms. Inhales deeply. After some beats, Joel enters with plastic and duct tape. Sees the group. Stops. Pause. Joel begins to tape the plastic to the window. Silence for some beats as Joel repairs the window. While working. Not looking at them. A sullen, tired, quiet sarcasm.)

JOEL. Carlo and Grace. The mould. The archetype of a good relationship. Such passion. And looks. Warmth. Humanity. Sharyl and I used to joke. Didn't we Sharyl. When we started to fall apart. When we still had a sense of humor. We used to say. That if we could. We'd have the two of you. Carlo and Grace. Bronzed into a statue. And put in our backyard. To remind us of happiness. *(Joel and Sharyl stare at each other. Then suddenly ... they both burst out laughing. Cathartically. Carlo and Grace stare at them in horror. Offstage, the baby cries. They stop laughing.)*

SHARYL. This wasn't supposed to happen.

GRACE. Then why did it?

SHARYL. We hoped it would be different tonight. *(Grace is shell-shocked. Her eyes dart around the room. Silence.)*

GRACE. I'm *very* uncomfortable right now. *(Pause.)*

SHARYL. Go to sleep. We'll have crepes and coffee in the morning. Forget all about it. I'm going to bed. *(Silence. She dims the room's light.)* Good night.

CARLO. Night.

GRACE. Good night. *(Sharyl goes up the stairs.)*

JOEL. The bed, as you know, pulls out. *(Pause.)* Linens in here. The refrigerator is yours. *(Pause.)* Good night.

CARLO. Good night.

GRACE. Good night. *(Joel and Sharyl leave up the stairs. Carlo and Grace stand frozen. Carlo snaps out if it, pulls the coffee table away from the bed. Grace stands. Does not move for a while.)* That's not fair. That's really not fair. They may be unhappy. But it isn't fair to put us through that. *(Carlo goes over to Grace. Hugs her. From upstairs, we hear Basso Nova music. Carlo and Grace instantly freeze and both turn to the stairs.)* They're playing ... that music. *(The baby cries louder. Carlo then begins to open the linens.)* I can't sleep with that music. *(Carlo snaps open a blanket. Carlo tucks the blanket into the bed corners.)* Ask them to turn it down.

CARLO. What?

GRACE. I can't sleep with that. Can you? *(Carlo looks up the stairs, then at Grace. Carlo hesitates.)*

CARLO. You really want me to ask? *(Carlo looks up the stairs. Goes to say something up the stairs. Somehow can't. Looks at Grace. Carlo looks up the stairs. Pause.)* Would you mind? Turning that down please? *(The music stops. After some moments, the baby stops crying. Silence.)* What? *(Carlo then begins to fluff a pillow. A beat, then looks up at Grace.)* Let's both try to calm down, sweetie. *(Carlo turns off the light.)*

GRACE. Do you love me?

CARLO. Of course I love you. That had nothing to do with us. We're not like them.

GRACE. Hold me. *(Carlo hugs Grace again.)* What happened to them?

CARLO. They've always fought in front of us.

GRACE. Never like that.

CARLO. They don't understand each other anymore

GRACE. Maybe they never did.

CARLO. I would never speak to you that way.

GRACE. I would never either. *(They kiss.)*

CARLO. And it was very sweet of you to talk me up like that in front of them.

GRACE. Well. I'm just … proud of you.

CARLO. Let's go to sleep.

GRACE. I'm going to sit here. I need to calm down.

CARLO. You're gonna sit there?

GRACE. Yeah.

CARLO. I'm gonna turn off the lights.

GRACE. Go ahead.

CARLO. You're just gonna sit there in the dark?

GRACE. What? I do it all the time.

CARLO. You sit in the dark?

GRACE. Yeah.

CARLO. I didn't know that.

GRACE. Well, I wouldn't do it if you were awake.

CARLO. Why not?

GRACE. I wouldn't have my privacy. *(Pause.)*

CARLO. You sit in the dark? *(Pause.)* And what?

GRACE. I don't know. Think.

CARLO. About what?

GRACE. I don't know. Things.

CARLO. What sorts of things?

GRACE. I don't know.

CARLO. Well, give me an example.

GRACE. Don't get upset.

CARLO. I'm not upset.

GRACE. Motherhood.

CARLO. What about motherhood? *(Silence.)* Come here. *(Silence.)*

GRACE. Do you ever think about fatherhood?

CARLO. Of course I do. But not in the dark. *(Silence.)*

GRACE. I sit. And I drink tea. And I think. And watch you sleep. Then when I get drowsy. I put my tea down. And I grope my way to the bed. And I put my head on your chest. And you groan for a second. And I say shhhhhh. And I think about. How I like to watch you watch me watching *you* shave. Or how you sit at the bar on some of my restaurant shifts. And watch the stock brokers flirt with me. Or how I sometimes slip out of the apartment. To buy you flowers at the deli at three A.M. Because they're cheaper then.

CARLO. And how you leave them on the kitchen table. For me to see when I get up. *(Pause.)*

GRACE. They're not like us. They don't understand each other. Maybe they never did. How could they? How could people who understood each other treat each other like that? If they did understand each other, if they did truly love each other, how could that happen?

CARLO. I love you.

GRACE. You do?

CARLO. I love you so much.

GRACE. I love you too. *(They kiss and start to undress each other.)*

End of Act One

ACT TWO

2002. The living room of Grace and Carlo's small New York one-bedroom apartment. A massive photograph of an infant on one wall. Grace and Carlo are conspicuously underdressed.

GRACE. I have to say. It's a little strange, to have you turn up at our doorstep like this.

JOEL. I know, it / was very short notice …

SHARYL. We didn't plan on dropping in like this.

GRACE. I would have prepared something.

JOEL. We came to New York for a romantic weekend.

SHARYL. On impulse.

JOEL. We do that a lot now — travel on impulse.

GRACE. Must be nice.

JOEL. See some shows. Visit the old restaurants. We weren't really planning on visiting anyone.

SHARYL. But then at Le Fou.

JOEL. Yes! Le Fou. We ate there tonight!

SHARYL. We thought of you!

JOEL. We couldn't resist. After all these years. It was still delicious.

SHARYL. And then I said what if we just …

JOEL. Dropped in … *(Pause.)*

GRACE. Right. *(Pause. Joel and Sharyl look at each other.)*

JOEL. And. We thought. We thought you wouldn't see us.

SHARYL. We wanted to make things … better … between us.

JOEL. We didn't get a Christmas card from you for the last two years. And you really didn't return any of our calls.

SHARYL. We thought this was the only way we could see you. *(Silence.)*

JOEL. *(Gets up.)* We won't overstay our …

CARLO. Are you kidding? Stay as long as you want. Spend the night with us. *(Grace shoots Carlo a quick look.)*

GRACE. What?

JOEL. No no no no no.

28

CARLO. Please.

JOEL. No no. We have a hotel room. To be honest, we're dying to get back to it. *(Silence.)*

CARLO. Well, it's good to see you guys again.

SHARYL. Is it? You'd think after last time.

CARLO. We all have our days. We're glad you didn't … you know.

SHARYL. Didn't? You can say the word. It's not taboo.

CARLO. Divorce. *(They chuckle awkwardly.)*

SHARYL. We are too. Glad. Glad we're not divorced. We're very happy now. A year of couples therapy. A long vacation to Thailand. Joel is in AA.

JOEL. Things are. Things are better. *(Sharyl smiles.)*

SHARYL. They are. *(Joel and Sharyl kiss passionately. The intercom buzzer buzzes.)*

CARLO. Oh. We ordered shakes. *(Carlo exits. Grace lights a cigarette near the window. Looks outside.)*

GRACE. Is that your limo out there?

JOEL. Yes.

GRACE. With the driver waiting?

SHARYL. We've been out all day.

GRACE. He's just sitting out there.

JOEL. Yeah.

GRACE. Just waiting for you.

JOEL. Do you want me to invite him up? *(Carlo enters with two shakes.)*

CARLO. *(Offering to Joel and Sharyl.)* Here. Take them. I insist. *(Joel and Sharyl take the shakes after a beat.)*

GRACE. What did you tip the guy?

CARLO. Enough. *(Grace picks up the receipt.)*

GRACE. The change?

CARLO. It was two milkshakes.

GRACE. Fifty cents is not / a tip.

CARLO. I rounded up / to the dollar.

GRACE. That's embarrassing.

CARLO. Am I supposed to give the guy twenty percent?

SHARYL. Yes.

GRACE. Why not? Why be stingy over some milk-shakes?

CARLO. *(To Joel and Sharyl.)* Please stop her, will you.

JOEL. It's kind of amusing actually.

CARLO. Oh, I'm glad you're entertained.

GRACE. The poor guy makes no salary. Probably an undocumented worker. Rides his bike out here in the pouring rain.

CARLO. Oh all right all right! It's drizzle.

GRACE. Look / outside. RAIN. Not drizzle. For *YOUR* milkshakes. And you tip him some /*change?*

CARLO. *SHHHHH.* Shh. Shh. Shh. *(Joel and Sharyl laugh. Carlo picks up the phone.)* I'll call him back.

GRACE. Call him back *what?*

CARLO. I'll order two more shakes. And I'll give him twenty bucks. Would that make you stop? *(Dials. To phone.)* Hi. Yes, it's 105 West Twenty-fifth. Apartment 2C. I'd like to order two more shakes. Yes. The same.

GRACE. *(Shakes her head.)* What a little boy. *(Joel and Sharyl chuckle.)*

CARLO. *(Hangs up.)* Done. And I heard you call me a little boy. So. Wow. You're really here.

JOEL. *(To Sharyl.)* Can you imagine what these two must think they're in for? After last time?

CARLO. Ah please / come on.

JOEL. The next apocalypse.

GRACE. *(Smiling, looking out the window.)* Well, to be honest …

CARLO. *(Brushing it off.)* Come on, we're no saints. We all have our marital stuff.

JOEL. Stuff? Good God. That's a nice way of putting it. It was sour *shit.*

CARLO. Well you know. With children. The stress. And worries.

GRACE. We said we would never see you again. *(Silence. Carlo laughs nervously. Joel raises his eyebrows, embarrassed.)* Well, didn't we? *(Pause. Carlo shrugs, then nods yes.)*

SHARYL. We came here tonight. *(Takes Joel's palm into her hands. Awkward, tense.)* To apologize.

JOEL. Yes.

SHARYL. We behaved …

JOEL. Horribly.

GRACE. You did. *(Pause.)*

JOEL. Yes.

SHARYL. We can't tell you how sorry /we are. We never planned for that to / happen. No please let me fin … We really didn't want or plan … for it to go the way it did that night.

JOEL. We're really sorry.

CARLO. It's fine. Please. Come on. You're our oldest friends. There's no … Come on. It's *fine*.

SHARYL. *(Pause. Now changing the subject.)* These shakes are delicious!

JOEL. Yes, they are.

CARLO. We like them.

GRACE. We order them a lot. *(Grace picks up the receipt. They laugh.)*

CARLO. So how's the baby boy?

JOEL. Getting to be less and less of a baby.

CARLO. Big?

JOEL. Unbelievable. He's with his grandparents this week. Who are very happy, mind you. We finally had him baptized last week.

CARLO. Did you?

JOEL. We broke down. Felt he needed to be … What was it?

SHARYL. Anchored.

JOEL. Yes. That. Anchored. Wow. The words we use. Anyway, we finally did it. The poor child endured it well. Grandparents in tears. Happiness. Photos. Big dinner. Flowers.

SHARYL. It was all, actually, quite moving.

JOEL. It was.

CARLO. So now you're … anchored?

SHARYL. We even go to church periodically.

CARLO. You don't. You do?

JOEL. Not often enough. But yeah. We do. *(Pause.)*

CARLO. Wow.

JOEL. Yeah, I thought that would shock you.

CARLO. It does shock me.

SHARYL. Why don't you tell them the story.

CARLO. What story?

SHARYL. How everything changed.

JOEL. We were having a horrible fight one afternoon. And I went down to my bar. Had five double whiskeys back to back. And some beers to chase it. Two hours later, I'm driving like an idiot. In the country. Swerving all over the place. In tears. Sweating. A mess. By now. I honestly don't know where the hell I am. And I see a bluff. A beautiful little bluff. And on it, a small church. And I shoot the M3 up the gravelly road to the bluff. Still don't know how I made it alive up that road. And I stop. Look at the church sign. Confession happened to be open at that hour. I hadn't been to a confession in years. Not years. Decades. Not since I was a kid. So

31

I stumbled into a confessional. Slammed the door closed. I was so cocky. I thought it was funny. I was amusing myself. Behaving like a spoiled kid. And then ... *(Pause.)* I started crying. Told the priest I was drunk. That I was unhappy. I told him what a mess my life was. I sunk into the confessional. Sobbing. It was pathetic. And you know what he told me? *(Pause. Simple, deadpan.)* It's okay. It's okay. It's okay. Kept repeating it. It's okay. And I stayed there. In the corner of the confessional. And he waited in silence. Calmly. Patiently. Said nothing more. Nothing. *(Pause.)* I caught my breath. And I got up and left. I went home. And slept. *(Pause.)* That's it. *(Silence.)*

CARLO. You're not proselytizing us, are you?

JOEL. You? It would be a waste a time.

CARLO. Because that's the last thing I need now.

JOEL. Well, that was the turning point. I went cold turkey. We both went cold turkey. With the booze, the fighting, the venom. We went into therapy. Things changed. *(Pause.)* I never went back to the church. I don't even know where the bluff is really. I never even saw the priest. Some days I think I dreamt it.

CARLO. Dreamt it?

JOEL. It doesn't matter really. Because it wasn't the place. Or anything particular he said. It was the way he said what he said. His voice. Like I heard a voice from somewhere. *(Pause.)*

CARLO. Huh. *(Pause.)*

JOEL. I'll always owe that man something.

CARLO. Maybe it had nothing to do with the man.

JOEL. But it did.

CARLO. Maybe you just needed someone to listen.

JOEL. But who in the end did listen? Some voice in a dark confessional.

CARLO. Who was probably masturbating. *(Silence. They all look at Carlo.)*

JOEL. That ... That was inappropriate.

CARLO. Inappropriate? It was a joke.

JOEL. It's not funny.

CARLO. You used to think jokes like that were funny.

JOEL. Did I?

CARLO. So what are you saying, Joel? I mean — what? Was this — what? Super — natural? Other worldly? Are you — what? Telling me you had a ...

JOEL. It was just a guy's voice, Carlo. A guy on the other side of the confessional. He helped me. His voice. His voice helped me. *(Pause.)* I was about to kill myself, you know.

CARLO. *(Chuckles.)* Come on, Joel. *(Joel doesn't smile.)*

JOEL. What?

CARLO. Seriously?

JOEL. You saw me then.

CARLO. But people go through bad times.

JOEL. And people kill themselves because of them.

CARLO. Yeah, I know. But. *You? Joel?* I mean … are you serious? *(Pause.)*

JOEL. I had razors set / aside.

CARLO. Jesus / Christ.

SHARYL. Okay, let's change the / subject now.

CARLO. You were *that* bad?

JOEL. Sharyl? *(Pause.)* How bad was I? *(Sharyl says nothing. Looks down. Sadly moved, Joel and Sharyl gently hug. A mournful silence comes over the room. Carlo rubs his hands, then stares at his palms. Looks at Joel. Then back to his hands.)*

CARLO. I'm uh. I'm sorry. I … I didn't realize. Suicide is so … removed from me.

JOEL. You've never thought about it?

CARLO. Actually, no.

JOEL. Or dreamt about it?

CARLO. Uh, *no.*

GRACE. I've had dreams about it. *(Carlo turns to Grace, flabbergasted.)*

CARLO. What?

GRACE. Just dreams. You know, nightmares. I had one a while back.

JOEL. Really?

GRACE. I was in Buenos Aires. I remember the light. Not gold. Just lighter than gold. Full but not heavy. Like good music. Light and still full. And I walked all over the city. And somehow I … *(Smirks, embarrassed.)* I mingled with the whores.

CARLO. The *what?*

GRACE. Whores.

CARLO. The *whores?*

GRACE. The prostitutes. They all had lovely colored braids in their hair. And I smoked cigarettes with them. And they seemed to like me. And I told them I was from New York. And they thought *that* was wonderful. But I thought it was more wonderful. To be from Buenos Aires. Being from that light. From that music. From those smells. And the whores with braids in their hair. They fed me. And they gave me a place to sleep. And gave me two soft blankets. One for my top half. The other for my bottom. And they told me stories. And made me laugh. They told me how they loved Melville and Poe. And Whitman. And Elvis. And I told them I hated Elvis. And they asked me to take them away to New York. And I told them to keep me here in Buenos Aires. And then they told me of *their* dreams. And when they spoke of their dreams. The word itself stung me. And the next thing I knew. I was walking the streets of New York. Suddenly home. And the grief inside me. I don't know what it was about. But it was unbearable. And so on the subway tracks. At the Fifty-seventh Street Stop. Beneath Carnegie Hall. I jumped. *(Silence.)*

CARLO. You *what?*

GRACE. It was just / a dream.

CARLO. You *jumped?*

GRACE. Don't you ever have dreams like that?

CARLO. No!

JOEL. Come on, Carlo.

CARLO. I don't!

JOEL. You don't have terrible nightmares?

CARLO. Well I don't *tell* people about them!

SHARYL. Why not?

CARLO. Because they're private.

JOEL. We're friends.

CARLO. I don't want to know you had razors lined up. I don't want to know about the church on the bluff. The drunken sob-fest in the confessional. Or her Argentinean romp with the whores. These things are private. There is such a thing as privacy, you know. I mean, we can't all just go around *dangling* our ids. *(Pause.)*

JOEL. It was a big moment in my life. I felt I should share it with you.

CARLO. All right. Now. Stop. Okay. Stop — stop right there. Since when do you use such a phrase? *Share* it with you. What the hell is that, Joel?

JOEL. What don't you understand?

CARLO. Every time adults use that phrase. It's as if they've been

34

neutered.

JOEL. That church is where things turned around for me.

CARLO. My friends don't have religious conversions.

JOEL. Who said religious conversion? It was just a turning point.

CARLO. Same thing. And now your son is baptized?

JOEL. Isn't yours? *(Pause.)*

GRACE. No. *(Silence.)*

JOEL. Hey, don't look at me like that. I could care less.

CARLO. Right.

JOEL. I'm not judging you.

CARLO. *(Mimics.) Isn't yours?*

JOEL. That's not what I / meant.

CARLO. Right.

JOEL. Don't be so hard on me, Carlo. *(The men stare at each other. Sharyl stands. Looks at the photo.)*

SHARYL. Your son. I mean look at him. Could he be more handsome?

GRACE. Thank you.

SHARYL. Those cheeks. Truly a Gerber baby.

CARLO. Every baby is a Gerber baby.

SHARYL. That's not true, actually.

CARLO. I think he's ugly. *(Joel and Sharyl look at each other, surprised, then laugh.)* It upsets her when I joke like that.

GRACE. Of course it / upsets me!

CARLO. It's a joke!

GRACE. You shouldn't joke / like that.

CARLO. Maybe what scares you is that I believe / it?

GRACE. Do you?

CARLO. NO! *(Joel and Sharyl laugh lightly. Grace doesn't.)* Am I the only one left with a sense of humor? *(Silence.)*

SHARYL. *(Motions to the room.)* Can I take a peek?

GRACE. He was fidgety tonight.

SHARYL. Who knows the next time we'll see him. Just one peek. I promise to tiptoe. *(Grace nods yes. The women leave. The men sit in silence. Joel gets up and looks at the photo.)*

JOEL. I like the photo.

CARLO. Huh?

JOEL. The photo.

CARLO. Oh. You want to buy it?

JOEL. Probably out of my price range.

CARLO. I doubt that.

JOEL. Oh whatever happened to the Romario Retrospective?

CARLO. It was cancelled.

JOEL. Why?

CARLO. Romario is a psychopath. His wife left him. So he pulled the show. And without him there was no show.

JOEL. Well, that sucks. (*Carlo looks at the door the women have just exited from. Then looks at Joel.*)

CARLO. It did suck. Do you get anxious when women pair off like that? (*Joel frowns. Doesn't know what Carlo's talking about.*) When they go do something that we *should* want to do. That we *should* like to do. Like go stare at a sleeping baby. Why do I want to stare at a sleeping baby? (*Pause.*) We should both go in there together later. As a joke. That would shock them. You say let's take a peek. And I say sure. And then I'll follow you in there. (*Joel smiles. Sips his milkshake, staring at Carlo.*)

JOEL. You seem a touch off, Carlo. (*Carlo looks up at Joel suddenly, defensively.*) You doing all right?

CARLO. I'm fine.

JOEL. Yeah? (*Pause.*)

CARLO. So now that they're gone. That story you just told us. It's just a story, right?

JOEL. What do you mean?

CARLO. It's me, Joel.

JOEL. Yeah *and?*

CARLO. You're not … like that.

JOEL. Like what?

CARLO. Epiphanies. Religion. Moments. It's not you.

JOEL. Look. It happened. I was moved. I'm sorry I told you. Obviously it upsets you.

CARLO. Of course it upsets me!

JOEL. Why?

CARLO. Because I know you. And years from now. You're gonna confess it was bullshit. Yes / you are.

JOEL. No.

CARLO. You're gonna / confess to me. That story / was a load of crap.

JOEL. No. It wasn't a story.

CARLO. Mark my / words.

JOEL. I'm incapable of having a spiritual moment?

CARLO. A *what?* A spiritual *moment?* In graduate school we took photos of rosaries wrapped around glowing dildos. We were angry at our catholic upbringing. We mocked it. A spiritual moment? *You?* What are you talking about, Joel?

JOEL. It was just a moment of poignancy. It was a tonic. Something / fresh.

CARLO. A tonic?

JOEL. Something that made my numb life mean something.

CARLO. And what does your life *mean* now, Joel?

JOEL. I don't know. Something. I'm trying to figure that out. I guess everyone is in one way or another.

CARLO. Not really.

JOEL. No?

CARLO. It's a luxury actually.

JOEL. What do you mean a / luxury?

CARLO. It's a wealthy man's luxury.

JOEL. Wealthy uh what? What is that supposed to mean?

CARLO. Most of us ... here on *earth,* Joel. Worry about the next grand to pay the bills. We don't have time to stare at our navels. And hear voices in confessionals. *(Pause.)*

JOEL. Fair enough.

CARLO. Oh you're agreeing with me now?

JOEL. Maybe there's some truth to that. But it's unfortunate. People have a right to more. We weren't put on the earth. Just to claw and scratch to stay alive.

CARLO. Joel. Why don't you ... *(Shakes his head.)* Joel, tell us ... Why *were* we put on this earth?

JOEL. Why are you an art photographer?

CARLO. It's what I do.

JOEL. That's the only reason?

CARLO. Is there another I don't know about?

JOEL. You tell me. *(Silence.)* If I'm spiritual at all, if I'm *religious,* if I can even say that with a straight face. And you know me. And my ironic past. If / I can do any of it. Without calling myself a fake. *(Pause.)* It's because of poignancy.

CARLO. Past? Because of *what? (Pause.)*

JOEL. *(Quietly.)* There are moments. When life distills itself tightly. For just a second. Something moves me. Something tells me that I can go on, that I should go on, that I want to go on. *(Pause.)* What is that thing? *(Pause. Carlo laughs. Joel doesn't.)*

CARLO. You're talking to *me*, Joel. Not some guy at the end of the fucking bar.

JOEL. Whoah, what *is* your problem tonight?

CARLO. My problem?

JOEL. You're fidgety. You're hostile. You've / barely sat down.

CARLO. Your problem is the real / question.

JOEL. I'm happier than I've ever been.

CARLO. What is that supposed to mean?

JOEL. What do you think it / means?

CARLO. Happier than you've *ever* / been?

JOEL. What don't you understand / about that?

CARLO. Fine. Fine. Right. Okay. Good. Fine. Let's stop. *(Silence.)*

JOEL. What's wrong, Carlo?

CARLO. Nothing.

JOEL. I know you.

CARLO. I'm fine …

JOEL. You can tell me / what's wrong

CARLO. I'm fine

JOEL. Fine.

CARLO. Just stop asking.

JOEL. All right.

CARLO. I'm fine …

JOEL. You seem …

CARLO. Money.

JOEL. Money? *(Carlo goes to the window.)*

CARLO. Grace and I. Our debt. It's crushing us. Grace had to drop out of grad school to work at the restaurant again. *(Looks at Joel.)* Remember grad school? All the loans. The credit cards. The nights out. We said it would all work itself out. Have you paid off your student loans? *(Pause.)*

JOEL. Yeah.

CARLO. I haven't sold a photograph in … *(Carlo laughs awkwardly. Shakes his head. Rubs his hand through his hair.)* Not one.

JOEL. I'm sorry to hear that.

CARLO. Not as sorry as my wife.

JOEL. Why don't you go into advertising? *(Pause.)*

CARLO. I told myself I would never do that. *(A loud car horn blares outside. Carlo moves away from the window.)* Credit agencies call us. Sometimes at ten at night, to catch us off guard, because they know we'll answer the phone. *(Silence.)*

JOEL. How much money do you need? *(Silence. Carlo doesn't answer.)*

CARLO. I wanted to call you. A few months ago. Grace wouldn't let me. *(The women enter.)*

SHARYL. So sweet. He was breathing in and out so fast. Did you miss me? *(Sharyl falls onto Joel and kisses him romantically. Carlo and Grace stand watching.)*

GRACE. Did the delivery boy come? *(Carlo nods no. Carlo and Grace stand watching them kiss. A bit more horrified this time. Joel sees them staring.)*

JOEL. Gross, right? *(Pause.)*

CARLO. Revolting.

JOEL. Sorry.

CARLO. No, it's fine. You seem so, so …

GRACE. Repaired. *(Joel and Sharyl look at each other, smile.)*

JOEL. I guess we are.

GRACE. So why did you have an affair? *(Pause.)*

SHARYL. Ooo, that's a big question.

JOEL. Ouch.

CARLO. Grace.

GRACE. What? I'm sorry.

SHARYL. No, it's fine.

GRACE. I thought. Since you were being so candid, you wouldn't mind … I mean, it wasn't a secret, right? *(Pause.)*

SHARYL. I wanted to destroy Joel

GRACE. Why?

SHARYL. I was repulsed by him.

JOEL. She was.

SHARYL. When you're repulsed by some one. You stop seeing them as a human being. You even imagine them as less than a human being. An animal. I looked at Joel … and saw … a pig.

JOEL. She did. *(A loud car alarm outside.)* That I don't miss about New York. *(Carlo closes the window.)*

CARLO. I'm beginning to hate this city.

GRACE. Beginning?

JOEL. You? Hate New York?

GRACE. That's all he does now. Complain about the city.

CARLO. Everyone out of work. Everyone terrified. And the rest of the country LOVES New York. It's disgusting. All over the world. Fucking T-shirts in Tapei. I LOVE NEW YORK. NOW

MORE THAN EVER. NYPD! NYFD! NEW YORK YANKEE HATS! TWIN TOWER T-SHIRTS! 9-11 COFFEE TABLE BOOKS! TOUR BUSES! STUPID PARADES! THE *TODAY* SHOW! *(Mimes waving to the cameras.)* ALL OF IT! REVOLTING! I was in New Mexico last month, I told a guy I was from New York. And he said, WOW THAT'S COOL. I asked him why is that cool? He said. I guess because *you were there.* And I said, why would being there be a good thing? And he looked at me, and he smiled, he did, he smiled — like I was a possession of his now. And he said, because ... *you* ... were a part of history. You know what I said? You're a *jackass.* Get out of my face. *(Pause.)*

GRACE. I still love this city.

CARLO. Well you were born here.

GRACE. So?

CARLO. You have to say you love it.

GRACE. I have to? That's a stupid thing to say. *(Pause.)*

JOEL. Can I take a peek?

CARLO. What?

JOEL. Can I take a peek?

CARLO. Can you *what?*

JOEL. Take a peek.

CARLO. Oh. Yeah. Sure. Let's go. *(The two men exit. The women watch them leave. And then look at each other, flabbergasted.)*

GRACE. What in God's name are they doing?

SHARYL. I don't know. Taking a peek. I guess. *(Awkward silence. Sharyl smiles. Grace smiles.)* So how are you, Grace.

GRACE. Good.

SHARYL. Good. *(Awkward silence. Grace begins to busy herself with clearing up the apartment.)* We're sorry about the last time, Grace.

GRACE. And how are you guys doing out there?

SHARYL. We're good.

GRACE. You seem so happy. *(Grace looks at Sharyl. Grace looks away and continues to clear up the apartment.)*

SHARYL. I want to make things better between us.

GRACE. So what have you been doing? Now that you have a nanny?

SHARYL. Well. I run the local arts council.

GRACE. That's nice.

SHARYL. I've been very happy with it, actually.

GRACE. *(Makes eye contact. Politely smiles.)* Good.

SHARYL. I've been meaning to ask Carlo … to maybe come in for a week. Run a seminar.

GRACE. I'm sure he would be flattered. *(Awkward silence.)*

SHARYL. I keep thinking about that trip we were going to take to Costa Rica.

GRACE. Really?

SHARYL. Would you be interested in …

GRACE. Maybe.

SHARYL. We had fun. The four of us. Joel says he misses that, misses you guys … *we* miss you guys. *(Silence.)* I almost forgot. This is for the little one. *(Sharyl hands Grace a wrapped gift.)*

GRACE. Oh.

SHARYL. He looks adorable up there.

GRACE. Thank you.

SHARYL. Well, do you want to open it?

GRACE. Shouldn't I wait to open it in front of the baby?

SHARYL. Oh.

GRACE. We usually.

SHARYL. Okay.

GRACE. That's what I.

SHARYL. Okay, sure.

GRACE. What I usually do.

SHARYL. Sure. *(Silence.)*

GRACE. Of course I'll open it. *(Grace hesitates. Then opens it. Pulls out a mechanical toy. Sharyl pushes a button on the toy. The women watch the toy move for some moments. They smile at it. Then at each other. It finally stops after some time. Grace smiles at Sharyl. Sharyl smiles back.)* Are you having any more kids? *(Silence.)*

SHARYL. I … can't have any more. *(Pause. Grace can't control herself … and bursts out laughing.)* Is that funny?

GRACE. Oh God. I'm sorry. I'm sorry. I'm just. I … oh my God. I'm sorry I laughed like that.

SHARYL. Is it funny to you?

GRACE. *(Still laughing.)* No no no no no. NO. It's just … you can't have any more, and I don't want any more.

SHARYL. So don't have any more. *(Grace's laughter stops. She stares out — stony.)* Oh.

GRACE. I'm not having it. I'm going next week. Carlo wants me to keep it. But we can't afford it. *(Pause.)* It's hard to admit. But I don't love being a mother.

SHARYL. It gets easier after the first three months.

GRACE. Oh don't tell me that. I'm not looking for advice. *(Grace lights a cigarette. Grace offers. Sharyl nods no.)*

SHARYL. Well what do you want me to say?

GRACE. Don't you ever get angry about it?

SHARYL. Angry?

GRACE. Taking care of your boy.

SHARYL. A little. But it passes. I'm grateful.

GRACE. Last week in the grocery story. I had had a long day. And I was in the cereal aisle, talking to my little boy. *(Grace begins to speak in a voice often spoken to infants. She speaks it at the new toy in front of her, as if she were speaking to her own baby. Her rage grows throughout the speech, yet she always maintains her affected "infant" voice.)* Oh, who's gonna eat those cute little tiny little toes? Oh, you are such a piece of flesh? *Who's* gonna bite those digits! And just gobble you up! Oh yes, *who's* gonna do that? *(Digs her face into the toy.)* Who's gonna take a *little* bite out of that *little* hand! *Ohhhh,* you think it's funny? Well, what if I just left you here right now? Don't you laugh at me. Don't you dare laugh at me. Oh, you won't think it's funny when I crack all your little fingers! Crack! Crack! *Crack! Crack! (Pause. Back to her regular voice.)* And then I looked up. And there were ten people in the cereal aisle staring at me. *(Sharyl doesn't know what to say. Grace smiles. Somehow this felt very good.)* Don't get me wrong. I love my boy. But some mornings, when I'm all alone in the shower, I commit myself to getting on the next flight to Buenos Aires ... and never looking back. *(The men enter.)*

JOEL. So cute. So sweet. Breathing in and out.

SHARYL. Go on. Mock me.

JOEL. I would never. *(Kisses Sharyl. Carlo puts his arms around Grace. Grace walks out of his embrace quietly.)*

CARLO. What were you guys talking about?

GRACE. Nothing.

CARLO. *(Only half cocky and sarcastic.)* Was Grace bad-mouthing me again, Sharyl?

SHARYL. Why would she do that?

JOEL. Did we surprise you?

SHARYL. What do you think?

GRACE. I'm stepping outside for a moment.

CARLO. Why?

GRACE. Because you don't have any more cash for the delivery boy. *(Carlo realizes.)* Yep.

CARLO. Shit. I spent what I had on the milkshakes.

GRACE. Yeah, you should have thought of that when you called him back here.

CARLO. I called him back here because of you! *(Joel kisses Sharyl.)* Okay. You *have* to stop doing that. It's *disgusting*.

JOEL. What? Kiss my wife? *(They kiss again.)* Kiss your wife. She needs it. *(They kiss again.)*

GRACE. I'm going. Anyone / want anything?

CARLO. I'll go.

JOEL. Just let me pay / the kid.

GRACE. No.

CARLO. No / no no.

JOEL. Why not?

CARLO. You can't.

JOEL. Why not?

CARLO. It was my —

GRACE. *Cheapness.*

JOEL. It's fine. Here's a twenty. *(Grace looks at Carlo. Carlo doesn't take it.)*

CARLO. *(To Grace.)* I was *not* cheap with the tip. I was reasonable. Cheap. Only you. *Only you* would use that word to your own husband in front of his friends. *(Picks up phone.)* I'll call him back. Tell him not to come.

GRACE. And embarrass / yourself again?

JOEL. Just take / the money.

GRACE. *(Leaving.)* Goodbye.

CARLO. I'll go.

GRACE. It's fine. Believe me. I need the air.

CARLO. No I'll — *(Grace leaves abruptly. We hear the door slam. Awkward silence.)* She's mad at me.

SHARYL. You think?

CARLO. What did she say when we left the room? *(Pause.)*

SHARYL. Not much. She asked if I was happy.

CARLO. Did she say she was *un*happy?

SHARYL. Is she unhappy? *(Carlo looks at Sharyl. Surprised at her forthright question. Then he looks out the window.)*

CARLO. So how's your house?

JOEL. We've added to it.

CARLO. What did you add? A moat?

JOEL. An alcove to the kitchen. Some more patio space. You should come visit. *(Carlo looks out the window.)*

CARLO. She's furious. *(Silence.)*

JOEL. Why not take the twenty?

CARLO. She's stubborn.

JOEL. So am I. Let's order two more shakes. And I'll pay. Call the guy. Tell him to bring two more shakes.

CARLO. You want me to call that man?

JOEL. He's coming anyway.

CARLO. You really want another shake?

JOEL. I want a shake. *(To Sharyl.)* Do you want a shake? *(Sharyl shrugs.)* Let's order two more shakes. *(Pause.)* So ... should I call?

CARLO. No no, I'll call. *(Leaves to the kitchen. Dials. Offstage.)* Uh ... hi. Hi. Yes, it's 105 West Twenty-fifth. Apartment 2C. Can we have two more shakes? Same, yes. Thanks.

SHARYL. Let's go.

JOEL. It was your idea to come.

SHARYL. I was wrong. *(Carlo hangs up and returns.)*

CARLO. He's already left the diner. They're gonna beep him.

JOEL. Oh / no no.

SHARYL. No they can't

JOEL. Call them. Tell them it's not necessary.

CARLO. I can't call them again.

JOEL. Well, we *better* tip this kid after what we've put him through.

CARLO. He's not a kid.

JOEL. What do you mean?

CARLO. You said kid. He's not a kid.

JOEL. Then what is he?

CARLO. Our delivery boy is an old man.

SHARYL. No.

CARLO. An old Mexican man.

SHARYL. And you *didn't* tip him?

CARLO. Don't tell Grace. She'll kill me. I would've told her. Had she not asked me. "What did you tip?" After she looked at the receipt. "What did you tip?" Every time we have anything delivered. "What did you tip?" I'm not a cheap man. I'm just not a millionaire.

SHARYL. How old was he?

CARLO. I don't know. Fifty. Sixty.

SHARYL. *Sixty?*

CARLO. Probably forty. He had gray hair. Maybe he hasn't aged well.

SHARYL. Of course not. He makes three cents an hour.

CARLO. So now you're going to lay into me?

JOEL. I have an idea. Why don't I ... This is gonna sound crazy. But I have a hundred-dollar bill in my wallet.

CARLO. *What?*

JOEL. Let's give it to him.

SHARYL. Joel.

CARLO. This is getting obscene.

JOEL. Why not?

SHARYL. Because it's patronizing.

JOEL. Why?

CARLO. Joel / no.

JOEL. Why is it patronizing?

SHARYL. Because it is.

JOEL. He needs money. Guy doesn't speak the language. Probably no education. Why does it have to be patronizing? Why am I the awful person here? Nine out of ten people wouldn't think of it. *Ten out of ten people wouldn't do it.* Why not a bit of generosity? Does that have to be called patronizing? It's not like we didn't get any help along the way, Sharyl. Where would we be without your dead grandparents? *(Grace enters carrying the milkshakes.)*

GRACE. Before I was angry. Now I'm fuming. HE'S FUCKING ANCIENT! AND you got more shakes out of guilt!

CARLO. No!

GRACE. Bullshit!

CARLO. *They* wanted the shakes!

SHARYL. Grace, we —

GRACE. Do you know it's raining outside!

SHARYL. We ordered more shakes.

CARLO. *They* ordered the shakes!

GRACE. A poor old man tramping about for your whims!

JOEL. Where is he?

GRACE. Gone. I paid / him. And tipped him.

CARLO. They wanted the / shakes!

JOEL. But *I* wanted to tip / him.

GRACE. Thanks, but I got it.

JOEL. But I said I would tip him.

GRACE. It's done.

JOEL. Here, take the money.

GRACE. No.

JOEL. Take it. *(Grace sees the bill.)*

GRACE. Are you kidding?

JOEL. No.

GRACE. That's a hundred dollars.

JOEL. I know you guys need it. *(Silence.)*

GRACE. Did ... did my husband ask you for money?

CARLO. What?

GRACE. Did he?

CARLO. I didn't ask ...

GRACE. You did, didn't you? *(Silence. Grace storms out into the bedroom.)*

SHARYL. *(To Joel.)* He ... asked you for money? *(Carlo exits to the bedroom.)*

JOEL. I can't stand the way Grace looks down her nose at me. *(Joel picks up the phone.)* I am not going home with that hundred-dollar bill. I'm calling that diner back. And that delivery boy is coming here. And I'm going to tip him this hundred-dollar bill.

SHARYL. What?

JOEL. I'm calling. Where's the redial?

SHARYL. We should leave now, Joel. *(Joel leaves and calls. Reenters with the phone close to his chest)*

JOEL. What's the address here?

SHARYL. How the hell do I know?

JOEL. *(To phone.)* I don't know the address. It's the place on Twenty-fifth that just had the milkshakes. Could you send him ... *(Pause.)* He hung up on me! *(Pause.)* Hello. Look, don't ... Well, I want you to send that old man back here. I'm serious. I want to tip him a lot of money. Fine. We'll do that then. WHATEVER. Just send him over right now. *(Sarcastically sweet.)* Thank you so much, sir. *(Hangs up the phone.)* Asshole. *(Joel enters.)* They didn't believe me. So I ordered four more milkshakes. *(Silence.)*

SHARYL. How much money did Carlo ask for?

JOEL. He didn't say.

SHARYL. He's always been irresponsible. Never managed his money.

JOEL. Oh let's not judge now. Who knows what's happened to them.

SHARYL. It's not a mystery. He's been in debt since we've known him.

JOEL. I was in debt once.

SHARYL. And we took care of it.

JOEL. Some people aren't as lucky, Sharyl.

SHARYL. Is that what this hundred-dollar tip is about?

JOEL. We're not going to fight are we?

SHARYL. Your luck? His lack of it? Showing generosity by giving a stranger a hundred dollars?

JOEL. He's not a stranger. He's the delivery … man.

SHARYL. We're not floating in money.

JOEL. No one ever admits. They're floating in money. If they did then they would actually have to feel guilty.

SHARYL. Guilty? We *earned* that —

JOEL. Oh don't start in with the meritocracy line, Sharyl. I / don't want to talk politics. You know we inherited money. And / I took a job I can't stand. A job that kills me day in and day out.

SHARYL. So! People inherit money all the time! We sacrificed. We moved away from New York. We made choices. How much does he want?

JOEL. He didn't say.

SHARYL. He didn't?

JOEL. We didn't get into it. We were interrupted.

SHARYL. Do you think it's a lot?

JOEL. You know. There is no difference between Carlo and I.

SHARYL. Oh please.

JOEL. We went to graduate school together. We had the same dreams. Same ideals. Don't look away. You know it's true. We did. And look at him.

SHARYL. So you're gonna give him money?

JOEL. If you agree, yes.

SHARYL. And if I don't?

JOEL. Then we'll talk about it.

SHARYL. And if after we talk about it and I still don't agree.

JOEL. We'll flip a coin.

SHARYL. Very funny.

JOEL. Then of course, no. No. We won't lend them the money. *(Pause.)* That would get them out of their crushing debt.

SHARYL. Oh please.

JOEL. Those were his words. Crushing debt. Poor guy.

SHARYL. He said crushing debt?

JOEL. Yes.

SHARYL. When someone says crushing debt — and asks for

money — they mean *a lot* of money.

JOEL. I think we should give them some money.

SHARYL. Why?

JOEL. They need it.

SHARYL. We don't?

JOEL. Not really, no.

SHARYL. I don't agree.

JOEL. You know we don't, Sharry.

SHARYL. So then let's give away *all* our life savings to friends, beggars, delivery boys! Good! *(Grace and Carlo enter. Silence.)*

CARLO. Sorry guys. *(No one knows what to say.)* Grace says the delivery man speaks perfect English.

JOEL. Really?

GRACE. I started to ask him. Do you have any change? And I stopped mid-sentence. Realizing he probably didn't speak English. And he said, I have change. And I said. Oh you speak English. And he said. Of course I speak English. Why wouldn't I speak English? And I said. My husband said you didn't speak English. And he said. Your husband's wrong.

SHARYL. *(To Joel.)* Still want to tip him a hundred bucks now?

JOEL. Yes, why not?

SHARYL. He's coming back.

GRACE. He's coming back?

SHARYL. He called him back.

CARLO. You called / him back?

JOEL. I did what I said I was going to do. Tip the man a hundred dollars. He's coming back for the tip.

GRACE. You called that poor old man back here?

JOEL. To tip him a hundred dollars!

SHARYL. For some reason, my husband wants to show his generosity this evening.

JOEL. Sharyl. *(Silence. Grace can't hold in her words.)*

GRACE. *(To Joel.)* You must be enjoying this.

JOEL. Enjoying what?

CARLO. I thought we said we / were done fighting.

GRACE. You are.

JOEL. Enjoying what, Grace?

GRACE. Him, groveling. Look at your smug face. You love this, don't you.

SHARYL. And why is that?

JOEL. What the hell are you talking about?

GRACE. This is your revenge.

JOEL. Revenge?

CARLO. Grace. Please you have to ...

JOEL. No, no, no. Revenge for what?

GRACE. For your mediocrity. *(Pin-drop silence. Finally ... Joel bursts out laughing.)* He was the more talented of the two in graduate school.

JOEL. Oh my God.

GRACE. In fact you had very little talent. If any at all, and you had an inferiority complex for years about it.

JOEL. Did I?

GRACE. Yes, you did. My husband got all the attention. He was the star of that graduate program.

JOEL. That he was.

GRACE. And this is your revenge, isn't it?

JOEL. I had an inferiority complex?

GRACE. You did.

CARLO. Grace.

GRACE. And this now. Oh, it must be delicious for you. To see him so weak. So needy. How powerful you must feel.

JOEL. So I harbor an inferiority complex? And I'm without talent? Is that what I'm supposed to believe?

GRACE. They're not my words.

JOEL. Well whose are they? *(Slowly heads turn to Carlo. Silence.)*

SHARYL. This is why I don't like dinner parties. *(Pause.)* All this baggage. Beneath everything.

JOEL. Well it's not *beneath* anything *now,* is it?

CARLO. Why are you doing this?

GRACE. Because you're groveling. And I can't bear to watch it.

SHARYL. Let's go to our hotel room, Joel.

JOEL. I have to tip the delivery man.

SHARYL. Joel.

JOEL. First *you* ask me for money. And then *you* insult me.

GRACE. You loved it that he asked you for money.

JOEL. I did not!

SHARYL. Grace, he didn't.

JOEL. I actually wanted to help.

GRACE. We don't *need* help. We can get through this ourselves.

CARLO. Can we?

GRACE. This is between you and me. No one else.

SHARYL. How much money did he ask for?

GRACE. That's none of your business.

SHARYL. I think it is. Your husband asked us for it.

GRACE. Well, he's rescinding his request.

CARLO. We need fifty-five thousand dollars. *(The room goes quiet.)*

GRACE. What are you doing?

SHARYL. Believe me. Your husband doesn't need to rescind *any-thing*. Because / there's no way in hell ... Excuse me?

JOEL. Okay. *(Silence.)* Okay. *(Joel takes a long sip from his milk-shake.)*

SHARYL. *What?*

JOEL. I'll give them the money. *(Joel takes a long sip from his milk-shake.)* You've thought of me as talentless? All this time?

GRACE. Tell him the truth, Carlo.

CARLO. I thought of you as ...

GRACE. The *truth*.

CARLO. LET ME SPEAK! *(Pause.)* An underachiever. Wasted ... talent. You let me down.

JOEL. I let *you* down?

CARLO. So much potential and —

GRACE. OHHH *PUHLEASE!* YOU SAID TALENT*LESS!* PERIOD. OVER AND OVER TO ME! HAVE A SPINE!

SHARYL. Grace, you know, if we were honest like you're being, we wouldn't have any friends. *(Pause.)* What's a marriage without the gossip you share with your spouse. You should respect that gossip.

GRACE. Don't worry, Sharyl. We're not taking your money if that's —

SHARYL. I'm not talking about money. God knows you're not getting any money. No matter what my husband says.

JOEL. I'm giving them the money.

SHARYL. I'm talking about manners. It's not like we don't talk about *you.* The first time you saw our baby. We laughed at your expense for a week. Remember how you fed Lucien? Right to his mouth. With your unwashed fingers. God, I remember so clearly. You scooped up the rice with your fingers. And laid it to little Lucien's lips. So natural. So endearing. So earthy. SO *DISGUSTING!*

GRACE. Okay, enough, Sharyl ...

SHARYL. No, please. Let me finish. The next / day over coffee, my husband and I laughed at you. What a load of crap, we said. It's bad enough, she's got such slutty taste in clothes, such borough fashion — I mean, what? Fish net stockings, short skirts and tattoos? Come on. But that she takes her hands, her unwashed hands, and feeds Lucien as if it were NATURAL to her. What a liar! What a phony! YOU WERE TERRIFIED!

GRACE. Okay, stop.

CARLO. Hey!

GRACE. Please stop now.

SHARYL. Grace is pregnant again. *(The room goes silent.)*

CARLO. You told her?

SHARYL. So don't attack us, Grace, because my husband can support a family. It's not our fault you're embarrassed for Carlo. And let me tell you the truth. Your husband isn't Pablo Fucking Picasso either. He's a snob. *Always* telling Joel about *this* photography exhibit. Or *that* painter who's doing *this* in New York. As if my husband doesn't read the trades. As if he isn't wishing he were here doing those exact things.

CARLO. I don't tell you those things, Joel to look down on you.

JOEL. You do.

CARLO. Is that what you really think?

JOEL. Actually. You do.

CARLO. I don't. *(Pause.)*

JOEL. You do. *(Silence.)* Where's your checkbook, Sharyl?

SHARYL. My? No.

JOEL. Sharyl.

SHARYL. NO! *(Joel grabs her purse before she can get to it.)* What are you doing?

JOEL. *(Writing a check.)* I'm writing them a check.

GRACE. We're not taking that check.

CARLO. Why not?

GRACE. *(To Carlo.)* Because, you made a commitment to us. This is about *us*.

JOEL. Who else is gonna get you out of debt, Grace?

GRACE. Not *you*.

JOEL. Are you gonna call a bank? Ask for a loan? With what equity? Your restaurant job? His photos?

GRACE. I believe in Carlo's photos. He has an exhibit next month in New Mexico. It's just a matter of time. I believe in him.

51

JOEL. Well, it takes more than belief to sell photos.

CARLO. We'll pay them back, Grace. As soon as I sell something.

GRACE. Why would you take it from *them?*

CARLO. Because I deserve that money.

GRACE. Deserve it?

CARLO. Because what I say in my work is important. *(Pause.)*

JOEL. Wow. *(Finishing the check.)* Don't cash this right / away. I have to call my bank and make / arrangements. Please, Sharyl, I need to do this. And just so you know. I don't want this money back. It's not a loan. It's a gift.

SHARYL. Joel. No. *Absolutely* not.

GRACE. No.

CARLO. You'll get the money / back.

JOEL. Let me do this Sharyl.

SHARYL. Why?

JOEL. I need to.

CARLO. We'll pay you back.

JOEL. No. You won't. It's a gift. Or you don't get it. *(Grace picks up the check.)*

GRACE. We're not taking that money Carlo. *(Slowly hands it back to Joel.)*

JOEL. Why not Grace? Am I a mobster? Is the money dirty?

GRACE. No. It's just not ours to take.

JOEL. You know what I said? When he asked me for money? Why not work in advertising? And do you know what he said to me? I told myself I would never do that. *(Pause.)* I told myself I would never do that. Why would he say *that?* Why would he say that *to me?* Why not say ... I don't know. It's not for me. I'm not interested. I love what I do. I want to keep doing exhibits. I want to keep selling art. Instead he said. *I told myself I would never do that.* You see there's the line Carlo will never cross. Something he would never sink down to do.

CARLO. That's not what / I meant.

JOEL. That's *exactly* what you meant, Carlo.

CARLO. I meant that I have different plans.

JOEL. You have the same plans I once had!

CARLO. And you changed your plans!

JOEL. Maybe you should too!

CARLO. Why!

JOEL. BECAUSE THEY'RE NOT WORKING! And you shouldn't resent me for that! Grow up! Your plans! Your dreams!

They beat you down! They destroy you! Don't look at me like that! Ask any old man or woman. And they'll tell you the same. Even the successful ones. Let me fill you in Carlo. We're not brilliant. We're not special. We never were.

CARLO. There isn't a serious artist anywhere who doesn't think they're special. If they say otherwise, they're lying.

JOEL. I guess I was never a serious artist.

CARLO. I guess not.

JOEL. You think I don't look at myself in the mirror sometimes and want to scream? But I have a family now. And a place to live. And people I love around me. And a yard. Yes, a yard. Where my little boy can play. What more can I ask for? What more, really. At the end of the day. What the hell more can I ask for? *(Pause.)*

CARLO. It's not about wanting more, Joel. I want something different.

JOEL. Well, then there's a price. *(The buzzer rings. They stare at it. Joel walks over to it. Pushes it in. Silence. A knock is heard at the door. Joel picks up the hundred-dollar bill. Joel exits. Silence. Joel enters with four milkshakes. Hands them out. The four of them sip in silence.)*

CARLO. You gave him the hundred-dollar bill?

JOEL. Yes.

CARLO. What did he say?

JOEL. He stared at it. Took it. Looked at me. And said thank you.

CARLO. What did you say?

JOEL. I said you're welcome.

CARLO. How old do you think he was?

JOEL. Sixties.

CARLO. Do you think he was happy?

JOEL. Happy?

CARLO. About the tip?

JOEL. He smiled. I think he even bowed.

CARLO. He didn't.

JOEL. I think so.

CARLO. That's embarrassing.

JOEL. It was embarrassing.

CARLO. Are you glad you gave it?

JOEL. I don't know. *(Pause.)*

CARLO. Do you enjoy having money?

JOEL. Yes.

CARLO. When you have lots of it. What do you worry about?

JOEL. Keeping it. *(Silence.)*
SHARYL. I think we should go.
JOEL. Yes, it's time to go. *(Joel and Sharyl stand. Carlo and Grace stand. Joel hands the check to Carlo. Carlo doesn't take it. Joel places it on the coffee table.)* Good night.
SHARYL. Good night. *(Joel and Sharyl leave.)*
CARLO. Good night. *(Silence. Carlo looks at the check. Looks at his wife. Grace and Carlo stare at each other. No one moves.)*

End of Play

PROPERTY LIST

Wine glasses
Wine bottles
Large glossy brochure of photo exhibit
Telephone
Large fern plant
Blinds on window
Baby photo on table
Bottle of scotch and glass
Tray of crème brûlées
Butane burner
Plastic and duct tape
Bed linens, pillows, etc.
Cigarettes and lighter
Milkshakes
Receipt for shakes
Wrapped gift
Mechanical toy
Twenty-dollar bill
Checkbook and pen
Hundred-dollar bill
Ladies' purses

SOUND EFFECTS

Baby crying
Loud car horn
Loud car alarm
Door slam
Intercom buzzer
Sound of shattering glass from a window